GREEN

by Shirley Davis

DORRANCE
PUBLISHING CO
EST. 1920
PITTSBURGH, PENNSYLVANIA 15238

Dorrance Publishing Co
585 Alpha Drive
Suite 103
Pittsburgh, PA 15238
Visit our website at *www.dorrancebookstore.com*

ISBN: 978-1-6453-0153-0
eISBN: 978-1-6453-0734-1

GREEN

OCTOBER 11

She wanted to die fighting, but the last few minutes she was alive she gave up, she went limp, laid still but not yet dead. Before she was screaming, crying, swinging little arms and kicking little legs. I was holding her in the water. God! She just wouldn't quit and die. Stupid little shit!

The headline said, "Five-Year-Old Dies of Asphyxiation."

It was that little light green ribbon, tying back her brown hair. She had bangs, big brown eyes, a little square face.

I went over to Ed's.

"Hey."

"Hi. What 'cha doing?"

"Nothing much. Pam is pissed off at me. Kicked me out my own fucking place."

"Yeah"

I don't think he really gave a shit but asked.

"What for?"

"I needed some change and pawned her TV set. Only damn thing they would take."

"How much you get?"

"Fifty."

"Got any left?'

"All of it, I just did it...Why?"

Missy was watching TV. Her sister was there, but Missy had the little green ribbon. It just set me off. I could feel the hard on start.

'Let's go!'

"Let's get some hard stuff."

We drove to the Buffalo Bar to get a bottle, but we saw Russ and grabbed a barstool and had bar whiskey. Old Ed is a good drinker. So am I. We sit most of the afternoon, drinking until almost all the money is gone.

"Let's go."

"Let's get a bottle and go." I buy a quart of CLC whiskey and a six-pack of Coke.

That little green ribbon kept flashing me. I was trying, but the color would flash before my eyes and that would start turning me on. I like little girls. I like their tiny little twats. I like big girls, too. Pam was a good fuck. I just kept getting that flash of green and by now I was pretty revived. I see that green and get turned on.

"God damn, give me a drink!"

Hell! Ed wouldn't care. He probably did her himself. If not already, then soon. This kid is worth exactly the seventy dollar welfare check he gets for her and NO more.

Ed was snoring. He was passed out, the TV still on.

That kid is making me crazy...green...I am hard, throbbing and burning...got to...

"Missy! Let's go for a ride. It's a pretty night, look at that big moon, maybe we could go to McDonalds."

Hell! I can do her and dump her back here. Old Ed's gone. Why? That green ribbon, it's still there. Oh God, I have to!

She's crying!

She's yelling!

She's naked!

I took her underneath a big, old cottonwood tree, down by the river. She's still crying. I wrap the blanket around her and drag her on the ground, going up the steep bank. It is muddy, I am slipping backwards, sliding down some muck, try duck walking back up, dragging that crying little shit. I get to a barbed four wire fence and I try to throw her over, but she knows it and starts yelling, "No, no!"

"Shut up! You little shit!"

I smack her in the head.

"OHHH." A loud cry.

I toss her over the fence, holding on the bunched up blanket with one hand. Now I'm getting my left leg over. "Jesus!" I caught my pants, I am too tired and too drunk. I dropped hold of the blanket trying to pull pants off barb.

"Jesus Christ!" She's running!

I'm jerking and kicking my leg, harder and harder, my pants are still caught! She's running for the bridge! Oh Jesus!

My pants rip free. I'm running fast as I can. I have to catch her!

Got her! She is screaming, that shrill little girl, ear-splitting scream!

"Jesus Christ! Shut the fuck up!"

I grab her from the back and hit her hard as I can!

She's swinging her arms, her little hands are fists mostly hitting air and kicking her legs! I am holding her around the waist! I throw her over the bridge!

I hear her hit the water!

She isn't screaming.

I've got to get her, she will have to tell. She's all beat up now!

I run off the bridge, down the bank into the water. She's struggling and gasping. I grab her and hold her under the water.

She stops moving.

I think she hurts.

She doesn't fight.

She doesn't want to hurt anymore.

She is quiet.

I know she is still alive.

I keep holding her in the water.

Then... I know she is dead!

I let go. I look around. I see nobody and reach down to get her! "Fucking shit!" She's gone! I'm fishing around with my hands, reach all around my body, straighten up, turn around and then around again. Nothing! She is gone.

I climb up the embankment. I get into the car and throw it into drive. Whirrrr, the wick wheels are stuck in the mud. "Jesus Fucking Christ!" Now there is a pickup coming.

"Hey Man! You got trouble'?" Two guys in the pickup.

"Yeah, I'm stuck!"

"We got a winch. What the hell you doing here three fucking o'clock in the morning?"

Driving back to town, I am so hung-over, hungry, got the God-damnedest headache. I eat scrambled eggs and ham at the truck stop. I take a bunch of aspirin from the bottle I just bought.

OCTOBER 12.

The search for Missy used dog teams, professional man-tracking teams, and over four hundred other people from the two-state region. She was reported missing by her Aunt Peggy at 11:03 A.M. Dad and stepmom called Missy's mom, who was living with Aunt Peggy. The other kids were slapped and cursed, after they said Missy wasn't there. They all looked again, but said they still couldn't find Missy. Well maybe the little fart went to her mom's or maybe that crazy bitch took her. Aunt Peggy and her mom were anxious to have anyone look worse as parents than they were and quickly turned accusers and called the police.

Her body was found by Sam and Joe Bolder, about 7:30 P.M.. The brothers were volunteer searchers using their own rubber raft to float down the river. She was face down in five to seven inches of water. Naked with "pale foam" consistent with drowning She had several bruises, blood, but most noticeable between her little legs, anyone could tell she had been raped, her little vagina was torn and bloody, big purple blotches on her thighs.

OCTOBER 13

Pam and I plan a short trip. She's easy. I talk her into going to Denver, see a cousin of mine. They come for me while we are packing the car. I say I never met Missy.

"I never met that little girl, Missy."

"But you did know Ed."

"Yeah, I know Ed, off and on since we went to school together, but we are not best friends, nothing like that. No I never met Missy, last time I saw Ed, she was still living with her mom, I guess. It seems to me that I'm being framed, you know for something I couldn't do."

"Why is that?"

"I think, you know I'm being framed because it's an election year and they have to get somebody. I've got all kinds of friends that say I couldn't have done it. My family is behind me a hundred percent. You know I couldn't really hurt a fly except maybe with raid."

"What if the lab tests say different?"

"Just cause some screw up doc made me give blood. If that test comes back and says I did it, I can fucking guarantee it wasn't me that done it! I can fucking, fucking guarantee it! I am being framed!"

Authorities state the death of Missy is a sexual assault/homicide and the District Attorney said this morning he has a suspect in the case, however he does decline to identify that suspect. Autopsy showed sexual intrusion by object or penis and sperm was found. Several bruises had been inflicted both before and after her death and that she was alive for several hours after she was raped. State investigators have marked and casted footprints just upstream from the site where the body was found and near the bridge. Anyone having information please contact local police or call anonymous on the Crime Stoppers Hotline.

Doug Cattles is picked up for questioning. He is small in stature, 5'6", maybe 5'7", and thin, almost feminine bone structure, a long broad nose on an oval face. Light brown hair brushed back but normally loose and hanging about his forehead from a natural part in the middle of his head. He has a little upper lip and rarely smiles, his left eyebrow is arched giving him a "what" look. His beard is barely noticeable even when not freshly shaven. His eyes are light blue with bags under both eyes moving across and down his high cheek bones to make a V. Generally he looks unkempt.

As released from the State Investigators and District Attorney's Office

Yes, he was in the area where Missy's body was found, because his car got stuck when he was trying to get to a party at Piney Campground. He said he met six hunters in the Buffalo Bar that night, although he couldn't remember a name, but was sure they were from Kansas or maybe Nebraska. He said he was very drunk that night. He said they all wanted to go to the party, but not all six could fit into the hunters 4-wheel drive pick-up, so two rode with him. When his car got stuck, the two left in the pick-up to see if they could find a chain at the party. He was so drunk he fell asleep in his car. He awoke when the hunters tapped on his window about seven in the morning. Then he and the hunters drove to town. Later, he and a friend Mike Cole, tried to free the car but couldn't do it and had to call a towing service. Cattles said he attempted to jack up his car to free it and left the bottom of the jack at the site. When he returned to retrieve the jack stand, his car overheated due to a pin hole in the radiator. He stopped near the bridge and walked down the embankment to get water to fill the radiator and that's why police found imprints of his shoes along the creek bank. He said he tore his tennis shoes and pants while trying to get his car from the mud with the jack. His shoes were already worn out so he threw the old shoes and pants in some dumpster.

Doug admitted that he cleaned his car the day after Missy's body was found but said it was not to remove evidence. He also admitted he talked with acquaintances about an alibi for the evening of October 11 and morning of the 12th.

"I kind of paranoid out and started saying I needed an alibi. I told my neighbors to say my car was in the garage all night."

Doug Cattles says he is an alcoholic. He went to see friends in the Dry Creek area rather than return to his job as a roofer. He did not find them at home but at work on a drilling rig. He borrowed ten dollars from them to buy whiskey and bought a pint of CLC and put five dollars of gas in his car. He said he then decided, he was "going to be suicidal and end it all." He drove 98 mph on the interstate and attempted to hit the railing at the overpass bridge to kill himself. Instead, he knocked out the exit sign and three reflector poles and flattened two tires.

He drove on the rims for two miles to the Sports Bar and called Pam. He told her he tried to commit suicide. Then the officers arrived and took him in for questioning.

He said none of Ed's children should be with Ed. He said he visited Ed's home three times on the day Missy was reported missing to see if he could help find her. Ed said he had lost a daughter, but he still had four other children and he would only lose $70 off his welfare payments. Cattles said Ed showed no grief over Missy's death.

Cattles' preliminary hearing is closed to the public. His court appointed attorney filed a motion to close the hearing and the county attorney did not object. Judge's order states "from the circumstances, the information from the preliminary hearing would create a danger that a fair trial would not be possible. It does not appear that there exists any reasonable alternative to closure."

PSYCHOLOGICAL EVALUATION

HISTORY AND OBSERVATIONS

Doug Cattles is a thirty-year-old male, Caucasian, 5'7" tall, weighing 140 pounds. He was anxious and nervous appearing. He would fidget and glance nervously about the room. Throughout the entire assessment procedure eye contact was poor. He expressed himself well using adequate grammar and vocabulary. He engaged in no bizarre or inappropriate behavior that would suggest the presence of a florid psychotic process or severe depression.

He is currently on five-years probation for child abuse that he says was "just carelessness."

Developmentally, Doug presents a family history of severe abuse. He started running away from home at the age of seven and was independent by the age of fifteen. Doug's mother married his stepfather, who was extremely abusive, when Doug was one. Doug reports that he wet the bed all the time he lived in his stepfather's home. He would get a severe beating each time this occurred which turned into a nightly ritual.

I am not going to tell this quack that he fucked me in the butt over and over again and then beat me. The first time I was about five. He took me into their bed. Mom had on the bed those new green sheets she just bought. She loved green. She was always buying green this and that. He told me he would rub my back if I would lay on my stomach. So face down looking at that green it was pure pleasure. Then he found my dick and starting pulling it... Ohhh, still pleasure I liked it... I got hard. Then that old son of a bitch must have too because the next thing I knew he had his hard dick pressing in my butt crack. Then it hurt. He was on top and pushing that God damn, big old dick into my asshole. Jesus Christ it hurt! I felt my thing go limp and then he was off me. I didn't know it then, but he must have come and I must have come about the same time. All I remembered was first pleasure it felt good… then pain and pleasure and then really pain the old fart hit me on the butt, grabbed me, threw me across the room, picked me up, and slapped me silly and said if I ever told, this was just the start of what I would get. This was the first time…I think. A least it is the first time I remember.

At age eleven, he was committed to the state hospital. Doug states "I did nothing wrong."

"I swore to that old son of a bitch that if he touched me again I was gonna tell. He'd have to kill me and he damn near did.

He reports that his parents had him committed on the falsified statement of his little brother, Dale.

He made Dale swear that he never buggered him! He said I was crazy, using drugs and out of control. Hell, he never had no trouble controlling me on the bed with the green sheets, until I said NO MORE, and then I told Mom.

His relationship with his brother is conflicted yet today.

Doug has a spotty job history, according to Job Service records. He has worked as a roofer for about ten months, a sprayer for about four months and a hired hand off and on for a total of about two years.

A juvenile history of alcohol abuse and anti-social behavior is presented. He has been arrested for public intoxication, disturbing the peace and served three months in county jail for stealing beer.

Doug has a long history of multiple psychiatric symptoms that include derealization where he "feels like the events are happening to someone else" and depersonalization where it was like "watching a movie" of events in his life. Doug attempted suicide at the age of twenty-four, he shot himself under the chin and bears the scar. He has many symptoms of suspiciousness to the point of paranoid ideation. In discussing suicide, Doug states that he has no current intention, but "I don't give a shit." During the interview he made it quite clear that he was keeping many secrets and withholding information from the examiner.

The projective testing assessment indicated he is a sullen, angry, alienated, an oppositional individual. It is likely he is oversensitive to criticism and suspicious to the point paranoid ideation. A propensity to be selfish, self-centered, immature, grandiose and impulsive. During the assessment, he was suppressing lots of emotion, which was most likely suspicious, hostile, and resentful. He was feeling quite helpless, a victim of a hopeless situation that he was having a great deal of difficulty handling psychologically.

Being raised in a violent, out-of-control, dysfunctional family often results in a violent, out-of-control, dysfunctional individual interpersonal style. During times of escalating stress, his automatic response will be to revert to a regressive acting out manner.

DIAGNOSTIC IMPRESSION (DSMII)

Axis I   Alcohol Abuse

Axis II   Mixed Personality Disorder with Paranoid, Narcissistic, Compulsive, and

Anti-Social Features

<hr>

MAY 3

Doug Cattles pleaded not guilty to first-degree murder Thursday in Third Judicial Court. Cattles appeared nervous and shaky throughout the hearing but said he understood the proceedings and his voice was steady when he entered his plea. In court, the presiding judge cautioned Cattles against discussing the details of the case with anyone except his attorney. On Friday afternoon Cattles called the local newspaper to assert his innocence.

MAY 7

LETTERS TO THE EDITOR COLUMN IN LOCAL NEWS-
PAPER

I am writing with sorrow, devastation, and anger. In regards to five-year-old Missy, we need to protect our children.

So, tonight as you tuck your family into bed, picture your child in Missy's painful, abusive, and inexcusable death and then you can justify (her killer) being punished by death!

Doug Cattles this morning pleaded guilty to killing five-year-old Missy after kidnapping her from her home and raping her. The district judge, following a plea agreement between the county attorney and defense attorney, sentenced Cattles to life in prison on both the first-degree murder charge and the kidnapping charge and to forty-five to fifty years in prison for first-degree sexual assault. The sentences will run consecutively.